Progressive Gentle Horse Training

This book is intended to help you train the horses in your life.

When working with horses never advance your sessions beyond a level of your safety or confidence. If you are not fully prepared or confident with your ability to succeed, then please seek the help of a professional horse trainer.

Your safety remains your own responsibility.

I hope that you find this book helpful and that you and your horse learn to understand each other in a way that makes you feel blessed.

Take Care and God Bless!

ISBN: 1-4276-0061-9
Library of Congress Control Number:
To order additional copies, please contact us.
BookSurge, LLC
www.booksurge.com
1-866-308-6235
orders@booksurge.com

Contents

Introduction

Since God has allowed it, people have caught, tamed and trained horses to take a rider. Some do it with passionate, calculated skill and others have just died trying. Those who have captured an understanding and knowledge of the horse, to the point that they make working with horses look easy, are called "Horsemen".

People have trained horses for many reasons including personal transportation, delivery of cargo, fighting wars, putting out fires, tilling fields, driving cattle, sport and pleasure riding. Despite their inbred fear of predators, massive size, incredible speed and stamina, horses have always come to meet the needs of their masters (human beings).

Almost as vast as the uses that people have found for horses is the number of ways that they have learned to train them. Too many horse trainers believe that there is only one right way to train horses, which of course is their way.

In this book, I have taken some time to recap on some of the techniques that I use. I try to explain the techniques that work for me, in most cases. These methods that I share in this book are exactly the techniques I follow myself. My methods are an accumulation of techniques that I have learned from many horse trainers, whether through friendships , watching other horse savvy people, lessons, videos, or from reading books, magazines, and attending clinics and seminars. Some of these techniques are a slight modification or adjustment from what I've learned from other people. Together they are developed as techniques that I use and share with other people.

Since I do not consider my own techniques the only way, I am always learning, testing and adapting my techniques as I find the need to do so. I call these techniques my "**Progressive Gentle Horse Training**" methods.

The goal of this book is to introduce some of the methods I use to the reader, in a way that makes it easy to read and follow, and in a way that helps the reader enhance their own program.

As human beings, we have evolved to develop sophisticated tools and technologies to support almost everything we do. I think it's important that we learn to make use of some of these tools and the leverage they offer us. In this book, I will introduce the reader with some basic knowledge, concepts and techniques that work for me. My greatest hope is that clear, persistent and consistent use of the tools and techniques in this book will help you establish better communication with your horses.

Dedication

I would like to thank Terri, Jacob and Taylor (my wife and 2 sons), for their unyeilding support and encouragement in my life. They make all my hard work worth while and so much more enjoyable. I would also like to thank them for all their help along the way.

I should thank my Dad for helping me to get started in horses and for sharing with me his knowledge and his fun story's of his farm in Cuba. And my Mother for her faith in my success and her encouragement.

I need to thank Art Rios for his friendship and early coaching, as well as for taking me on as his apprentice as a farrier and for getting me started in a quality horsemanship program.

I would also like to thank every single one of my customers and clients for the generosity of their confidence in allowing me to work with their horses in the past and in the future.

I need to take a minute to thank the horses that I've worked with, for listening and giving me that "try" in every session. And even the ones that have kicked me, bitten me, run me over, dragged me, bucked me off and stepped on me for letting me live long enough to learn better ways.

I would like to thank my good friend Nicole King for helping edit this book with her new red pen and lot's of patience.

Lastly, I would like to thank God for the wonderful things he has allowed me to enjoy in my life and for the love and passion he's brought me.

Nature of Horses

The study of the horse has many references. Much of the rational thoughts on horses that we currently possess has been based on, or cultivated from, our knowledge, research and assumptions from how we see them in nature.

As we search our mind for answers to problems it is important to consider what we know about horses in general. It is also important to realize that even though our knowledge is a cultivation of efforts that we have already committed, we should remain very perceptive to all the variables of any problem we encounter, if we hope to fully understand it. In other words, if we want to understand horses we not only need to feed our knowledge, we also need to feed our senses and remain acutely aware of the details, signs, signals, and body language of the horse and our own body in order to make use of all that knowledge effectively.

Lastly, we should consider that even with all the knowledge that we have about horses and horsemanship the art continues to evolve. Every year people bring new knowledge, insight, or simplicity to our world with horses that benefits the horse and all his human partners.

Let's consider or review some of what we already know.

Horses are herd bound, vegetarian animals. Their natural diet consists mainly of grasses, bark, leaves, and water. They are a prey animal. Which means that they don't hunt other animals as a food source, but unfortunately they are hunted by other animals as a food source. I mentioned this early because there is no doubt in my mind that this is the most important thing that influences the horses behavior.

Horses have very long legs and a hoof structure that allows them to run very quickly over, through, around and across most types of terrain.

They have a large lung capacity and excellent muscularity that allows them to run long enough to evade most predators.

Horses have a long neck, a huge eye and large ears mounted at the top of their head. This allows horses to reach down to eat and drink while remaining ready to run away as fast as they can. It also allows them to lift their heads and spot predators at a great distance away. Their ears are directional (they can move each one independently) which allows them to fine tune their hearing, also enhancing their chances for survival against predators at a distance.

Horses are a free ranging herd-bound animal that can cover great distances of open range to support their life and diet. In the wild, horses learn to share pasture with other animals that are not a threat, such as, birds, deer and rabbits. Our observation of herds in the wild proves that while many horses lay in the sun and rest, others stand watch around the herd and at any instant, sharp sound or the snap of a limb can startle the herd into a flat out run.

Further study shows that often the herd is led by the movement of a single horse (usually the senior mare). This mare is usually a physically qualified mare but not necessarily the strongest or the fastest. She is, however, very keen to what the herd really needs to respond to. The accurate evasion of really dangerous activity is highly respected in herd animals.

The stallion's job is to cover(breed) the mares and to ensure the strength, speed and confirmation quality of the herds future. They are often an integral component of herd defense, willing to challenge and actually fight off predators with their feet and teeth as the herd gains distance in the direction of safety.

Foals are born rather quickly and ready to run with the herd in very short order. Survival of the fittest remains the rule. Eventually, they learn to sleep standing up and only require that deeper “laying down sleep”, on occasion. Almost everything that horses do is based on having the ability to run away.

In general, horses are quite content to live, eat, drink and play on the open range. They survive in many weather extremes from quite hot to below freezing temperatures. Horses in extreme weather eat more, move less, and find shelter from the wind. They really do not seek a roof over their heads in the wild.

The horse is also a highly social animal. Social structure lives within every herd. The strongest most agile horses secure their survival by holding their place within a pecking order. The Alpha horse is the highest horse in the pecking order; the Omega horse is the lowest horse in the pecking order. Let's talk about this for a minute because it is really important that we understand what it means to the horse.

First of all, the alpha horse gets to pick where he wants to eat and he keeps his position in the herd by successfully pushing the other horses around.

She (the senior or alpha horse) reaches out and bites at a junior horse's neck, shoulder, withers, back, flank or rump to push him away. Looking more closely we can see that she begins with a more gentle threat, she might start by simply flipping her nose twice at a horse that is closer to her than she wants it to be. She might then emphasize the threat by pinning her ears and baring her teeth at the other horse suggesting that she is getting aggravated and fully intends to follow through with a bite if necessary.

The responsive junior horse takes heed to this threat and backs off immediately; the less responsive horse or the horse that wants to ignore the threat will usually give a little pinning of his own ears back, saying “screw you pal, I was here first”. The horse that gave the warning will usually then follow up with a violent attack by biting the other horses head, neck, shoulders, back, or rump, or, by turning her rump towards the challenger and kicking violently with both feet. At that point the junior horse will either run away quickly, start flapping his gums in submission, defend himself by fighting back, or some combination of that assembly. Their short battle will confirm the leader within the pair. This battle doesn't normally affect the rest of the herd until or unless the junior horse moves up a rung in the social ladder. If that happens, the junior horse will normally follow up the confirmation of his new position by pushing the other junior horses on the ladder a time or two. Senior horses do not usually care about this change up unless the next senior horse realizes a potential threat to his own position and he feels the need to confirm his place by pushing the horse around that just landed right below him in the herds social ladder.

The senior mare that protects the herd with her ability to move them all, and keep them out of harms way, for that reason, she is given greater respect and seldom challenged. The herd leader is usually very highly sensitive to danger.

Stallions will battle for rights to mares, and that behavior is also somewhat separate to the normal balance of leadership. It is definitely one of physical strength, speed, and resilience.

So what is gained by this step ladder position of leadership? The senior horses get to pick their place in the pasture (normally surrounded by junior horses), this helps them survive a surprise attack by not being the first to get eaten. It also protects their foals in the same way. The senior horses also get the best wind break in cold weather and first drink in a shallow stream. This is all very critical to survival.

The Omega or junior most horses are instinctively (although sadly), more prepared to die. They are less aggressive and less resistant in the way they react to any threatening situations. They are also usually less fit and less exuberant.

Foals stick very close to their mothers. They move in sequence and learn their social skills from their mothers as well. It is actually quite beautiful to watch the harmony of movement between a mare and her foal in a pasture or herd situation. You can really get a taste for how accurately the foal can move and how closely they communicate with each other in flight, through their body language, by watching them for a while.

Foals of alpha mares generally live to establish their own position as alpha within a herd. Foals of junior mares tend to be less aggressive in the way of fighting their way to the top of the social structure of the herd.

The stallion can influence the foals greatly in their confirmation, attitude and confidence as well. Stallions that are athletic add to a foals ability to avoid the Omega position. A stallion that is strong and kind earns greater compassion from the rest of the herd and often receives less aggression by the general population. Stallions with greater stamina help secure the longevity and resilience of the foals which has a profound effect on the future of the herd.

If a prey animal understands that he is "prey", he will learn to fear the things that make him the most vulnerable (any surprise could signal the oncoming reward of a deadly fate). They develop fears that are intended to save their life. Things like fear of isolation (there is safety in numbers), claustrophobia (fear of capture), fear of the unknown (things that move or make a noise).

Although horses do have vocal forms of communications their primary form of communication is based on movement (body language).

The nature of the horse is something that every horse owner deals with whether they realize it or not. Whether we understand it or not. It is the basis for all equine behavior.

Whether we believe it or not, every human that walks into the heard (and is not considered predator or prey) gets sized up by the herd for their position in the herd. The herd decides where that human belongs (Alpha to Omega), depending on the humans ability to control the indivduals within the herd, and the movement of their feet.

Equine Body Language

Horses in observation all over the globe have been known to have patterns of communication. Many cowboys and scientists alike have documented these patterns of body language, squeaks, whinnies, and knickers. These patterns of communication are rather simple and cover the basic signals that horse trainers use to better understand a horses attitude, disposition, and emotions. I will share a few of those below.

1) **Head raising with a snappy quickness**. This is a reaction that indicates that the horse was surprised and wants to know more. If it is followed by a look right or left with ears turning and twitching then it is usually something farther in the distance. If the head comes up while you are holding the lead rope then it could also be an indication that the horse is fearful of what you want him to do and he is quickly considering his options for evasion (where can he run to).
2) **The horse prances with an arched neck** and head shaking gently from right to left (usually accompanied with a deep rolling nicker. This is normally the equivalent of todays trash talking. The horse is bolstering "I'm bad, oh yea, I'm bad". Usually this kind of behavior happens when a stallion meets a mare. It also happens when a confident horse meets a new horse or a happy confident horse is about to get some tasty grain (and he is glad to see you).
3) **Head comes down to the ground** as if the horse is sniffing the ground while walking or trotting, or even at a canter. This is a horse requesting

permission to meet and talk things over. It is sometimes (usually) a precursor to submission and sometimes just a signal that the horse is ready to find neutral ground to support co-habitation.

4) **The horse is licking and chewing** with his mouth open. This looks like a horse that gets peanut butter stuck to the roof of his mouth. This is generally a clear sign of submission, or at least a desire to stop and talk about things. The horse is saying "I give, I give, please don't hurt me". This doesn't mean that a more intense threat will not cause the horse to take flight, but, it is a clear signal of a desire to get along for now. This is often seen when a yearling is brought into a new herd.
5) **Pinning of the ears**, (when the ears lay back on the top of the neck). Most people know this one means business. It means that a horse is mad enough to bite you if you persist. A horse that pins it's ears around you is an incident waiting to happen and it needs to be trained to respect you and what ever your intentions are.
6) **A horse that walks toward another horse flipping his nose up and down** is saying you "better move out of my way because I'm coming through". This is a mild signal of aggression. It precedes the ear pinning, and the eventual bite.
7) **When a horse backs into you or turns it's back on you** or another horse (pointing it's rump on you), the horse is saying "you are in my space and, if you do not leave, I will consider kicking you". If the horse adds moving his rump towards you quickly and hunching down his rump then look out because he really means that he is about to kick you now.

8) **A horse that stands with one leg cocked**, (his weight is on three legs and he is resting his hip to one side)is relaxed.
9) **A horse that walks up to you, when you come in the pasture and puts his head down and toward you** (to offer his head), is both respectful and glad to see you.
10) **A horse that whinnies loudly** is trying to call horses or friends in a distance. It is usually associated with a separation anxiety.
11) **A horse that squeaks is bursting in emotions**. Usually this happens when two horses face off for a banter at the dominance game or a young horse runs with playful exuberance.
12) **Nostrils flaring and heavy nasal blowing.** This usually indicates that a horse is preparing for a requirement for expending energy. It is also a natural communication between horses that have just met to snort against each others nostrils, as if they were saying "You are in my herd now, so, let me know if you want to start something, I am ready if you are". Usually, one horse will show an additional sign of submission, other wise things might get a bit more intense and a squeak will follow.
13) **Eye wincing**, (a slow blinking of the eyes). This is usually a sign of pain or severe discomfort.
14) **Head bobs up and down while walking**, specially if the bob is rhythmic (ex. head comes down on the left front step and goes up on the right front step). The example would indicate that the horse was lame on his right front (head goes "down on the sound" foot).Watching the hip can indicate the same thing for a hind leg injury (down on sound).

15)**Mares that lift there tails and squirt urine**. This is indicative of a mare that is ready to be bred. Seasonal desires and fertility in mares can cause them to act a bit unpredictable around other horses.

16)**A horse that rears while backing away or turning away**. The horse in a pasture situation is providing a clear signal to the herd to run away. The horse with a rider or on a lead rope is saying that he is extremely nervous or afraid and he would like to run away.

17)**The horse that rears while moving forward** or closes the gap between himself or other horses is saying that he is trapped into a fight and ready to kick and bite. Usually pinned ears accompany this behavior.

18)**Tail swishing,** A horse that swishes his tail at you while you are brushing him down or picking his feet is trying to swat you away as if you were one big fly. It is a sign of irritation. It is also a form of disrespectful behavior. The horse that swishes his tail while you are riding him is also irritated and frustrated (not happy for one reason or another).

19)**The horse that opens his mouth as if he were yawning** (stretching his head and neck forward and possibly twisting left and right while doing it). This is usually a horse that is frustrated but knows he needs to remain submissive. It is kind of like a displaced aggressive behavior.

20)**Horses that are pawing the ground** (sometimes stomping), are unhappy or frustrated. Either they want out, want attention, want to be with another horse or they simply want their freedom.

21)**A horse that reaches his head around and pins his ears at you** when you are riding him is telling you that he is not happy about you pushing him along. He might also reach around and bump or nip your shoe with his mouth, indicating that you should just stay back where you are and let him take care of the ride.

There are other body language indicators that signal illness or discomfort, or even other less important communication signals but I will leave those for the medical journals. It should suffice to say that you should spend time understanding how your horse stands, how he sleeps, and acts around people and other horses so that you can quickly identify any irregularities in his behavior.

Understand that horses try to learn your body language and they try to communicate with you with their body language.

Humans in the Herd

Whether we realize it or not, whether we accept it or not, whether we want it that way or not, every time we walk into the pasture we join the herd. If we are not accepted as a herd member then we are a predator and the horses will not want a thing to do with us.

If we are accepted as a herd member then we will find ourselves on a rung in the social ladder. Where we land on that social ladder has a lot to do with the way that we communicate with our horses and how well we seem to get along.

If all we ever do, when we greet the herd, is feed or water the herd then we might take a different and somewhat obscure role in the herd as "**Herd Servant**". This is a role that is not found in the wild, it is the result of equine domestication and I will spend a minute or two on this now because I see it a lot.

The herd servant is the person that brings the buckets of grain, or the bails of hay or the hose to fill the water troughs. The servant might also on occasion lead the horse to the stall and blanket the horse in cold weather and muck out dirty bedding but the servant is not known for his / her ability to push the horses around or aggressively move any particular horse out of his way.

The servant has a tendency to always consider the happiness of the horses and their comfort first. The servant will walk around the horses so as not to bother or disturb them. The herd servant will always blame themselves for their horses misbehavior and dismiss it as something they should have seen coming. In my opinion, based on many years of helping horse owners with communication problems, this is one of the most common problems in the horse / human herd & domesticated equine behavior today.

Quite often the horse owner (the herd servant) does not acknowledge a problem until the horse in question decides to confirm his position over the servant human and the human failed to heed or listen to the warning signals.

Again, the owner tends to disregard the need for action until they get bitten, kicked, knocked over, run over, bucked off, or bolted on. Seven out of ten times the owner's reaction to this behavior is to put the horse away, feed them and go in the house for a good cry. Sometimes the response is to sell the horse to someone else. I'm sure you have seen the ads for the "bold horse that loves trails" , or the horse "for experienced riders only" (mis-represent any problems or a flat out lie about the horse's problems). Sometimes, (in more extreme cases) the horse will end up as dog food. On occassion, this is where a smart owner will hire a trainer to get some help.

As humans with horses (horse owners or handlers), we need to accept the fact that we have a responsibility to understand more about them. It is not enough to just find out what they eat.

The first thing we need to do is officially join the herd. We need to spend a few days and watch our horses.

Learn how horses behave with each other. Watch how they act when the sun is shining and the day seems perfect, watch them in the blowing rain, watch them when the water barrel is empty for a couple hours and when it gets refilled. Watch them when they eat grass, or how they behave when hay is tossed into the paddock in a couple piles. Watch them and note which horse is the most dominant (pushiest) and which is the most submissive.

Carefully watch the body language of the horses in all those situations and how they move their head, ears, rump, etc. Note what a horse looks like before he bites another horse, or what a horse looks like before he kicks another horse. This is critical to understanding the language of horse.

Much like the fact that you would not want to move to a community where communication was impossible, you would not want to try and join a herd of horses before you know the basics of their communication system.

We can reflect back on normal herd requirements and behavior to better understand this. Most of us get lost in our own wants and needs and we forget that we are not horses and horses are not people. Our wants and needs are different. By nature, we could not be more unlike the horse if we tried. I have never met a horse that spoke English or Spanish or successfully passed an SAT exam. They can not learn by reading a book or simply receiving a set of verbal instructions.

We can not teach horses to learn our language very effectively until we understand their language. We can not successfully teach or train our horses if we do not know their language, and we can not successfully manage our horses unless we learn the way that they (themselves) communicate.

Yes, I realize the repetition in what I am saying, and it is the “key to success”! We need to learn how they will respond to our behaviour and suggestions.

Horses do not need the most expensive grain that money has to offer, nor do they need free access to unlimited grass.

Horses do not need a blanket in 40 degree weather nor do they care how much it cost you.

Horses do not need to have their water trough cleaned daily (or chlorinated or streilized) nor do they understand or appreciate the work associated with washing the floor daily.

Horses do not need brass handles on their stall doors nor do they care what material anything is made of.

Horses do not need a sterile barn to live in, nor will they feel very comfortable in such a place.

Horses do not need to have their mane combed daily nor do they appreciate how pretty they look to us.

Horses do not need to have the barn isle polished, nor will they appreciate being able to see themselves when they look down.

In fact, our nature is so different that many of the things that we do to show that we care for our horses can contradict what they really need. We have a tendency to think that if we have a beautiful barn with large stalls our horses will be happy. My experience has told me that horses with large pastures, and a sturdy three-wall, run-in type shelter (that effectively breaks the winter wind and rain) are by and large the best kept horses (the bigger the pasture and shelter the better). When pasture space is not available, obviously you do what you can, but exercise, fresh air and sunlight must be a large (big) part of every day.

An average horse with a 10 x 10 stall is not any unhappier than a horse with a 14 x 14 stall. They could care less really because too much time in any stall will dull or aggravate a horse. It may even cause things like abscesses, muscle atrophy, stall coughing, cribbing, and other serious problems. Stalls that hold urine and never get mucked are nasty and smell nasty to us and we can't imagine that a horse would like to live in it. Because we want to keep them cleaner and we do not want them to live in their own feces, we can safely assume that it's a good idea to muck the stalls out daily and try to have enough adequate bedding to absorb or drain urine. However that steps in his own feces is not a horse that needs to be rescued.

Sometimes we can take this stuff too far!

A horse that has a clean 14' x 14' stall every day, could be far worse off than a horse that gets adequate excersize and lives in a small paddock and gets put in a 5' x 8' tie stall every night.

Remember, they would probably rather not be in there in the first place. A common problem is a concrete stall with a slick rubber mat and a coat of shavings that is far too thin to absorb a significant amount of urine. We do this because it makes it easier to clean and less money is spent on shavings. It can cause us to try and keep a sterile environment (bleach washed). This also kills helpful bacteria, and weakens a horses immune system.

It would be better to find a different solution or keep them outside if adequate bedding is too expensive. If you do keep them in a stall, then do it right. Clean it, but do not streilize it. Pick out their hooves several times a week and give them daily exercise and sunshine. Horses can slip and hurt themselves in that concrete or rubberized environment very easily. An environment that is too sterile will spoil the horse, negatively affect his immune system and could cause more frequent bouts of colic or a lack of ability to fight infection and illness naturally.

Stalls also need to be clear of sharp objects that can hurt the horse. Check for this often.

To get back on the subject of humans in the herd, let me just say this; we need to do the things that help them learn how to accept our leadership, our way of life, our safety requirements, and to safely tolerate our objectives. The most important thing a horse needs is an owner that cares enough to learn how to make sure he is taken care of properly. An owner that takes responsibility for his horses behaviour and training, exercise and care. A horse needs an owner that is not afraid to seek help or knowledge when they need it.

This will include teaching them to behave for handlers in all situations. Teaching them to stand quiet for farrier and Veterinarian care. If they stand quiet for their handlers then their handlers can do a better job, safely! This is our responsibility and if you do not know how to make a more responsive horse then read-on or get a trainer to help you learn.

Ground manners are critical for all horses. If we ride our horses then their behavior (while riding) is clearly important for our longevity and theirs alike. If we do not ride them then their ground manners are no less impoortant. The better we teach them to behave, the better their chances are in life.

I have seen many horse owners suggest that their mares do not need to be perfect because they are just broodmares. I find that to be an interesting theory, because I want the mothers of every horse I bring into the world to be a great educator of manners to the foals they produce. I think broodmares (especially) need to have great ground manners. On the other hand, if we don't take responsibility for leadership in the herd then we are indeed setting them up for failure, injury, and possibly premature death (as their next owner may end up euthanizing them). A foal that is not taught to lead safely is going to

suffer a lot of anxiety, fear, pain, and quite possibly, self-inflicted injury just trying to get along in life. A simple trim can feel like a life threatening thing to a horse, and an aggressive attempt to escape the farrier can result in a serious injury to horse and human. A horse that is improperly trained or infrequently handled or ridden can misbehave on the trail and cause a serious injury to his rider or even inspire an inappropriate beating from the handler.
Therefore, establishing human leadership in the herd and teaching your horses good ground and saddle manners is the most important component of a quality care program for horses. The good news is that human training is very easy to obtain, and proper human training can consistently produce good horsemanship and horse leadership skills.

Teaching your horse to respect you and behave in different situations does not require a special gift or sixth sense with horses. It only requires a can do attitude, a sound plan or program, and time. Almost anyone can do it.

I want to step back with an appropriate disclaimer at this point. Sometimes a horse can be too much for the handler. By that, I mean that the horse handler is not at a level in his horsemanship that he can successfully lead or train the rank horse.

I recommend two potential solutions for this problem:

1) Have a professional trainer work with the horse to a point where you can handle him. My experience tells me that this only works if the handler/owner gets involved and understands what the trainer has done and how the horse responds to it.

2) Trade the horse (sell it and buy another), for a horse that better suites the horse handlers/owners ability and desire. Remember that your only chance for providing an adequate environment for sound horses is to take a leadership role in the herd and accept responsibility for the actions and behavior of every member in it.

What Horses Really Need

So, what do your horses really need? The basic requirements are easy to identify but depending on why you have a horse this answer can become more of a challenge. I will try to capture the basic concept first and then answer a few other scenarios to build a better field of considerations for most horses. Keep in mind that I am talking about domesticated horses hear, not wild horses.

I think all horses need these things:

1) The number one thing that all domesticated horses need is an owner that has enough knowledge to keep them safe and healthy.
- That includes adequate food and fresh water.

- A safe environment that is structurally safe.
- Shelter from extreme elements.
- Manners, exercise, and cooperation/tolerance.

2) The number two thing that a domesticated horse needs is manners / tolerance when handled by humans.

3) The number three thing that a domesticated horse needs is patience / tolerance when something out of the ordinary is happening (some level of confidence – despooking).

5) The horses fifth requirement is regular exercise.
- Self motivated or enduced (remember they are flight animals).

6) The next thing that a horse requires is regular hoof care from someone with adequate knowledge in caring for a horses feet.

7) The next thing that a domesticated horse needs is access to an equine dentist at least once every couple years (often more frequent visits are necessary).

8) The next thing that a domesticated horse needs is an adequate vaccination and deworming program.
- Some cowboys might argue with this one but an annual visit by a Vet is a good idea.
- A sound deworming program is also a good idea, talk to your Vet about what that means in your area(it may vary).

Once these things are taken care of a horse has a good chance to live a long and happy life in domestication.

Let me talk about additional requirements in greater detail.

Let us say that you have a horse to show in dressage.

1. Your horse is going to need training in trailering (because he's never really left the confort of your farm).
2. Next your horse is going to need training in taking a rider. This training could require a good trainer or coach and a couple hundred hours of work.
3. Your horse might also need to attend a few shows that you do not plan to enter because you want to help him get used to the crowds of people and the strings of other horses at the event. The first few shows might be quite a challenge without preparation.
4. Next your horse is going to require adequate rest from the activity that you have asked him to perform, to prevent him from resenting the routines or souring to dullness.

Notice how my list might seem a bit different from the one you have been building in your own mind. It is easy to think about the things you need (like a new saddle, or a fancy bit, or a flashy bridle) and forget that the most important thing you need sits between the horses ears.

It is easy to think, "I need a bigger stall" or expensive, heated, water buckets or a nice pair of $400 boots, or a new set of clippers,etc..

The truth of the matter is that the horse really does not need a lot of what we waste our money on. He does not need a $60,000 barn, or that brand new Kubota Tractor, those are things we want. We may think we need a barn if we live in climatically challenging places, and that might help us committ more time to our horses (in that case by all means).

Basically, the horse needs proper handling, food, water, and exercise. He needs enough of it to be reliable and safe for his sake and ours. Trade nothing over these simple requirements. A safe horse gets better attention.

Even a slightly pushy horse can crush our toes with a bad step, or bite off an ear if he gets a little upset at supper time. He can also injure our farrier or much loved veterinarian. We need to take responsibility to give him the training and handling that he needs on a regular basis and provide for his basic needs.

These facts can not be over emphasized!

We need to realize that horses require constant and persistent maintenance. Know your horse and you will know what he needs.

Know Your Horse

One of the things that almost no-one does, but I find to be of extremely high value is a personalized horse profile. By annotating, measuring, or photographing what you can identify about a horse in normal (healthy) conditions we can then have something very tangible to compare it to when we suspect that a problem may exist.

What should we look at in our horses?

1) **Posture** - Know what your horse normally looks like!
- Does he hold his head up or down?
- Are his ears perked or droopy?
- Does his tail hang steady or whip like crazy?
- Are all four legs straight or offset in his stance?
- Are his eyes bright or droopy / half closed?
- Is his coat bright and smooth or patchy, ratty and dull?
- Are his nostrils clear or runny (quiet or flaring).

2) **Expression** - Know a happy normal expression for your horse.
- Again ears. eyes, nose, head and neck position?

3) **Appetite** - Normal or not interested?
- Is water disappearing faster than normal or slower?
- Is he leaving it behind or dropping a lot of it?
- How much water is consumed daily?

4) **Manure -** Know what's normal?
- Is there fungus, worms or any abnormal color changes.
- Is it firm or loose?
- Is it dry or slimy?

5) **Limbs** - Every time you go out to your horses eyeball his legs.

- Are there any new cuts, scrapes, or swellings?
- Is there new resistance to movement (as in leading)?
- Are there any signs of gimpy behavior?
- Is there a good look to the length and angle of the hooves?
- Are they too long or severely chipped?
- Do they hooves have a foul rotten egg smell or seem thrushy?
- Do the hoof walls look smooth and symmetrical or are there cracks, chips, or rings to ask the farrier about?
- Are the shoes on snug and straight?
- Does the frog appear full and healthy?
- Note the rhythem of the head and hips in movement (mentally or in a video).

6) **Vital Signs** – Know what your horses normal indicators are like so that you have something to compare it to if anything looks off.

- Check vitals often until you can remember what normal sounds / feels like.

Temp:

Adult horse at rest = 99 to 101

(103 and up means you have a problem)

Pulse: - Check by holding your index and middle finger:

1 – artery above the fetlock
2 – artery inside the jaw bone
3 – artery in the divet above the right eye.
4 – Use a stethoscope behind the left elbow.

Adult Horse at rest is 30 to 40 beats/ min.

Newborn: can be up to 120
Two weeks: up to 100
4 weeks: Up to 70
Yearling: from 45 to 60
2 year old: 40 to 50

Respiration: Average Resting Adult horse is 8 to 20 per minute.

- Respiriation probably should not exceed the pulse.
- watch the ribs.

Capillary Refill: Normal is about 1 to 2 seconds.

- pressing the finger on the gums (remove finger and count).

Skin Pinch / Hydration Test: normal rebound is immediate.

- Skin pinch test.
- Grabbing a fold on the skin of the neck and let it go, it should pop back immediately after release.
- If not he's probably de-hydrated.

Gum Color Check - look at the color of the gums.

- Very pale might indicate anemia or blood loss.
- Grey or white could be shock.
- Yellow Gums indicate liver problems.
- Bright Red could be a Toxic condition.
- Bright and Pink Healthy normal.

7) **Lung Sounds** - Pick up a cheap stethoscope.
   - lungs should sound clean
   - no rattles, wheezes, or gurgles.
   - Check from the rib cage where your leg would be.
8) **Gut Sounds** - Silence is not golden.
   Place your ear or stethoscope high on the flanks.

- You should here pipes, gurgles, rattles (digestion).
- Silence could mean a stop or blockage in the works.

Once you know what your horses "normals" are then you should start thinking about how you can make keeping horses easier.

Find a program to follow to improve your horsemanship.

Any program from a reasonable source will do. I personally like the methods of most "Natural" or "Gentle Horse Trainers". I believe in any program that works to improve the horse human communication while keeping as it's top two objectives safety for the horse and human, and improvement in communication.

Set up a 40'-60' round or oval corral close to the barn, that has a well drained footing (sand or grass). I like having a small arena or round corral very close to the barn or run-in shelter that the horse lives in because it helps make it easy for me to keep up with the horses exercise and ground work maintenance.

If my horse has no ground manner issues then a larger arena works fine but I need to saddle the horse up and ride him at least 3 days a week (keep in mind 5 to 6 is best). A horse with a job makes for a happy horse, I believe that a horse or human that feels useful sleeps better at night.

Learn how to use a rope-halter and lead rope to lead and work a horse from the ground. This obviously goes along with the prior statement that proper regular handling solves most horse behavioral problems.

Keep clean, good quality, food and frost free water sources protected from climatic extremes and safe from mold, and mildew. You might have a barn with a loft where you keep your hay and keep it stocked so that it's easy to pitch your horses their feed.

If you are not sure about the quality of your hay, then you might consider sending your hay out for analysis. You can find links to hay test facilities from my web sight at www.blacksteedacres.com. It is nice to have a regular source for consistency in quality.

I suggest that you make arrangements with a local farmer and work with each other to maintain a healthy lifelong relationship. Avoid getting hay from too many sources.

Do not use feeders that are mounted high, horses need to eat and drink from low sources. They are not like a giraffe that eats from tree tops.

Run-in shelters are easier to maintain than barn stalls. The key is that horses know when they need to come inside. Confinement is unnatural for horses. If you do keep horses in stalls then the need for regular exercise becomes even more critical.

Check your horse's vitals on a regular basis to know when things do not seem right. Check your horses hydration levels, the way he walks, the brightness of his eyes, and his breathing patterns as well as his temperature, breath rate and pulse.

A good idea is to have a blood test when the horse is normal and have it filed with your veterinarian for later comparison when you suspect that he might be sick. You might also consider and discuss with your "vet" some of your options for moderate vaccination and deworming in your area.

Work on your horses manners at least 3 days a week. Regular ground work will help you get a good look at your horses health and attitude as well as help him to remember how he needs to act when on the end of a lead rope.

Pick your horses feet out at least 3 times a week. It is a good idea to pick out muck and dirt, while you check for nails and stones, and get a good look at his growth patterns.

Check your horses environment regularly and ensure that the horse can not be cut or injured by anything.

Take a walk through your barn and pastures. Look for nails, splinters, spikes, toxic plants, sharp siding, loose fencing, or boards, etc.. Fix it or get rid of it.

Make sure that your horse exercises daily, whether it is a 15 minute frolic in the paddock a couple times a day or a calculated lungeing from a lead rope.

Horses need to move for proper circulation and digestion.

Understand your horses needs by checking them often and consulting professionals.

Progressive Gentle Horse Training

When I talk about "Progressive Gentle Horse Training", I am talking about a method of training horses that is gentle to the horse and progressively improves cooperation, respect, trust, and communication between people and their horses.

I have spent a large part of my life studying the techniques of many great horse trainers and I have seen, studied, and tried the effectiveness of many different techniques (tried and tested them on many horses). I have also spent a significant amount of time watching horses. What I gravitate to is the use of techniques that work best for me in "most" situations. That is always where I start.

Sometimes it is exactly as I have planned it and sometimes I need to try different things until I start getting the response I am looking for.

Trust me, even though horses all speak the same language not every horse will respond like every other horse to every technique we use. For that reason, you have got to start with a reasonable plan and if what you are doing is not working, simply adjust your plan. You might have to take a step back and take a little more time getting a better grasp on the previous lesson. Honestly evaluate your steps and allow your horse to tackle something simple that works toward your goals. This approach will also serve to help him build his confidence in you and his trust in you as you consider your options in moving forward.

By using the word "gentle" what I mean to say is that, at no time, do I plan to use a force or pain to make the horse do anything. That does not mean that if a horse tries to run me over he will not get a sharp smack from the end of my dressage whip, it simply means that I will not smack him as a planned technique in my training program.

Progressive Gentle Training encourages horses to become more tolerant to things that are out of the ordinary. In that process the horses begin to get more familiar to responding to simple cues. These simple cues in-turn become a new form of communication between horse and handler. That communication builds trust and confidence. That new found trust and confidence builds comfort and peace of mind. Comfort and peace of mind builds joy and happiness. And with all those things working for you communication also gets a bit more clear.

Stand in a safe place, away from striking distance from any feet, and keep the horses nose tipped towards you. This keeps him from being able to turn his rump on you and kicking you.

Start easy by getting the horse to move his feet. Ask the horse to move away from pressure by using rhythmic pressure and progressively teaching horse to move away from it. Use a dressage whip and rhythmically tap him on the rump. Use the rope and swing it rhythmically at the horse's rump. Always reward the slightest progress.

We strive to always start any request with the lightest pressure possible and gradually build to what ever intensity is necessary. We keep three goals in mind with every technique and lesson. This is called "sensitization". The horse becomes more sensitive to moving away from certain cues and pressure.

We also teach a horse to be less sensitive to things that normally scare them (out of their mind). We do this through a process of gradually introducing things that scare them (things that move or make a noise).

We can start by introducing things that are the least scary and expose them to the horse over and over until he stops responding to it (as he stops responding to it we stop introducing it), that way the horse teaches himself to be less sensitive to those things. This type of training is called "desensitization". Gradually we introduce more scary objects until nothing scares our horses into wild flight like behavior.

What you will discover in this process is that with proper use of these techniques the horse will find a point where he lets go of his fear, he lets go of his resistance, he lets go of his objection and he puts some faith and trust in you. That is the exhale, the magic moment when he is willing to learn and accept your training.

Things to keep in mind:

1) Our own safety is the number 1 priority.
2) The horses safety is the number 2 priority.
3) We must reward the slightest try or slightest progress.
4) Always remain as gentle as possible but as firm as necessary.

In this book, I hope to share, with great detail, some of the techniques that I use to help horses and handlers better understand, and accept each other.

Getting A Horses Respect

Control the movement of the feet and you will control the horse.

The first consideration when ever I work a new horse is my safety. To safeguard my safety I need to start by working on getting his respect and trust before I can ever focus on any other problems. I start every session with this in my mind.

Let's spend enough time on this subject to really understand it. It is the most important part of every horse / human relationship, or training program, and it can solve about 75% of all other problems.

So before we can understand how to get a horses respect perhaps we should consider what disrespectful horse behavior would look like. Here's what I see in disrespectful horses.

1) The horse pins his ears when you come around.
2) The horse runs away from you even if he's wearing

a halter and you are at the other end of his lead rope.
3) The horse runs around you while you are leading him, paying attention to everything but you.
4) The horse pushes you with his head or shoulder and tries to get you to move.
5) The horse uses you as a scratching post for his head.
6) The horse walks into your leg while you are leading him (repeatedly) and fails to stop when you stop.
7) The horse nips or bites at you if you do not go where it wants you to.
8) The horse stomps his feet or rears up while you are holding the lead rope to scare you off the line.
9) The horse turns it's hind quarters on you when ever you try to get near it, or when you enter the stall.

Now, these are some of my observations when dealing with disrespectful horses. That said, I should also add that in many cases fear and disrespect draw a fine line. I try to consider that the horse may be both afraid of me and disrespectful. That way I can cover all the bases.

Let's begin by getting a horse's respect. Since we have not worked on any forms of communication, we need to get started by using something that the horse understands.

We are going to have to dip into our knowledge of herd behavior if we plan to gain any ground here.

We mentioned earlier that an alpha horse confirms or asserts its leadership by getting the other horse to move out of its way. So, if we can control the movement of a horses feet then we can assume that the horse will consider us higher on the social ladder than itself.

What do we mean by controlling the horses feet? We can start by suggesting that we control his movement forward, backward, left and right. Let us keep it simple at first and in later sessions we can consider sideways movement in both directions and finally movement with no direction (piaffe – very advanced control).

Here is where we need to think things through a bit. We need to ask ourselves a few questions before

we get started. We need to first make sure that we believe that we can safely proceed. If we do not feel prepared or ready to face the challenge or if we feel that the horse is too large or too wild or too rank then a good alternative is to hire a professional trainer to help get things started.

Watch and work with the trainer to get a feel for it. Study the horse and the trainer until you feel ready to take over. I like to start with longeing in a controlled environment (such as a 50' round pen).

I actually start by free lungeing in most cases because I want to let the horse run unrestrained if fear is indeed the cause for mis-communication. It also helps me prove to the horse that I mean him no harm. As soon as I get the horse in the pen I disconnect the lead and send him off running with a wave of my hands or a swing of the rope.

Standing in the middle of the pen, I let the horse run in one direction along the fence line. If the horse stops I toss the end of the rope towards the horses rump (or wave the whip at his hind quarters) and ask him to continue. I am chasing him forward. I am, in a sense, controlling the movement of his feet in a forward direction.

The round pen is a place that is very dependent on body language. Picture this if you will. Moving in the round pen you should walk very relaxed, as if the horse's running has no impact on you. Looking at the horse intensely causes his feeling of pressure to increase. Moving towards the horse, but behind the girth-line, causes the horse to move forward.

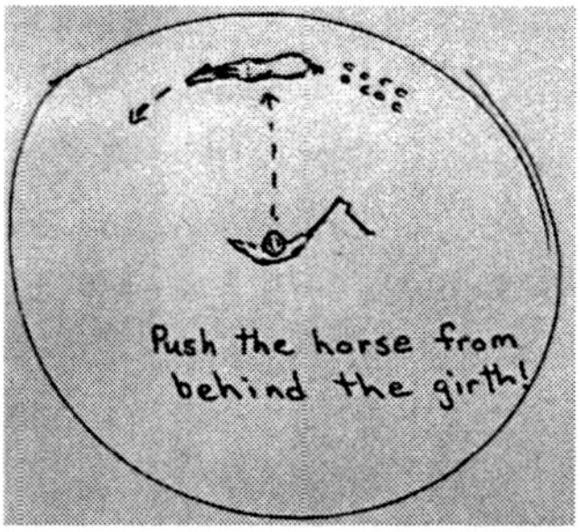

Moving towards the horse from the side, but in front of the girth chokes off his forward movement and pressures him to turn-around and run in the other direction.

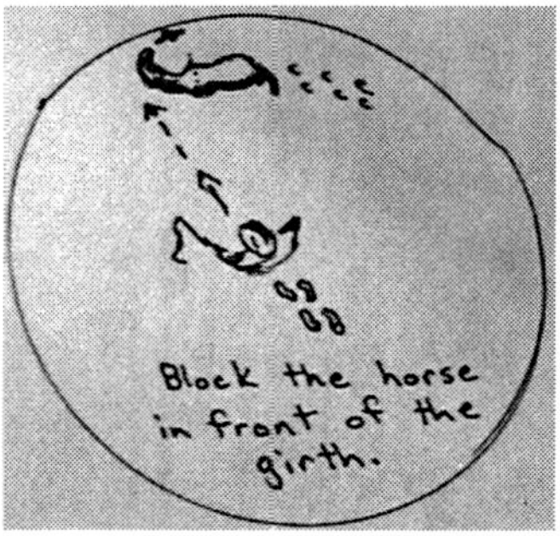

If we step away from the horse, we draw him into the center (toward our movement) of the pen. If we move toward him we push him away.

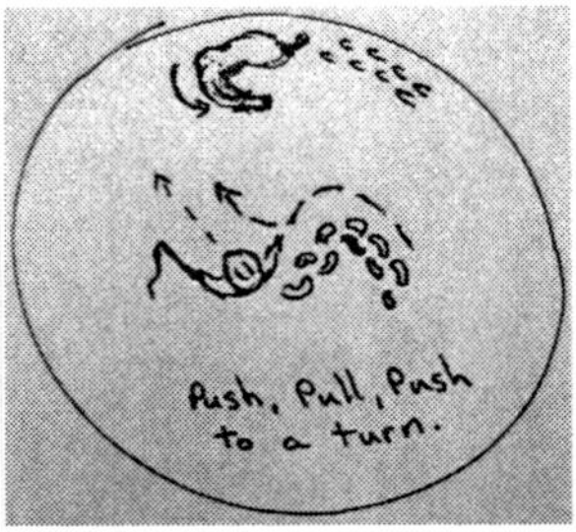

If the horse turns away from you, he is, in a way, showing you his rear end and it could be considered disrespectful, or, simply an evasion. Don't worry too much about that in the beginning. In the beginning his energy will be high and he might be just a bit more afraid of you so this is expected behavior. I like to see him run about 5 good laps in one direction then I close him off by moving in on him, in front of his girth line.

He will usually slow down and turn away from me by turning into the fence and heading off in the other direction. I let him run another four or five laps. If the horse tries to stop in these initial laps I chase him off again by waving my hands or tossing the lead line toward his rear end.

NOTE: When I say that I toss the rope, what I mean is that I hold one end of the line and toss the other end toward the horse (scare him with it a little). I usually toss it towards his rump to keep him moving forward.

Soon (if things are working as planned), you will see the horse move in less of a panic, I suggest that you reward that behavior by working a bit more gently (relax a bit in your posture and movement). Watch the horse very closely for signs in his body language. If his nose is pointed away from you as he runs then he's probably trying not to think of you as his leader. Usually the first sign of change will be that his inside ear will turn towards you (he is starting to listen to you). Soon you will see the horse dip his nose as he runs the circle. This is actually a sign of early consideration of submission. Your horse is suggesting that he stop running and negotiate a new cooperative contract with you (he's suggesting that you try and find some neutral ground). I usually wait until I see the second or third dip of the head (it will look as if he were sniffing the ground as he runs). At that point I will take my eyes off of the horses head and stop encouraging him to move out. I will turn my shoulder and eyes away from the horse in the direction that he is moving, thus taking pressure off him and encouraging him to draw himself toward me and take a little break (my body language is very passive at that point).

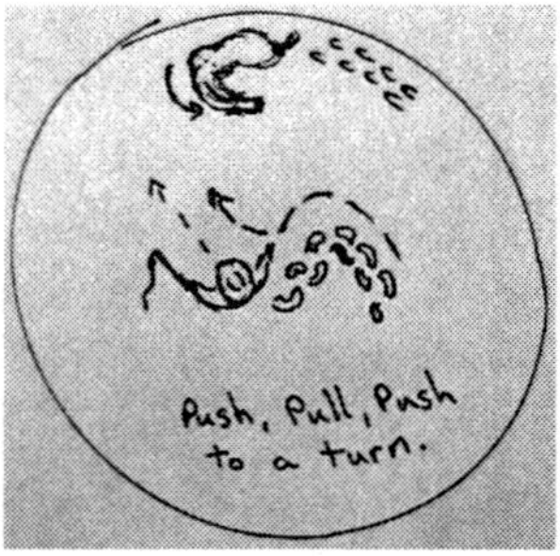

Again, the second that the horse looks towards me I turn my shoulder away from him and turn 180 degrees away from him for two or three steps. His movement should stop and my activity will have a tendency to draw his body in toward the center of the pen. I will know things are going well if he takes a couple steps away from the fence and approaches in my direction licking and chewing (another clear sign of submission).

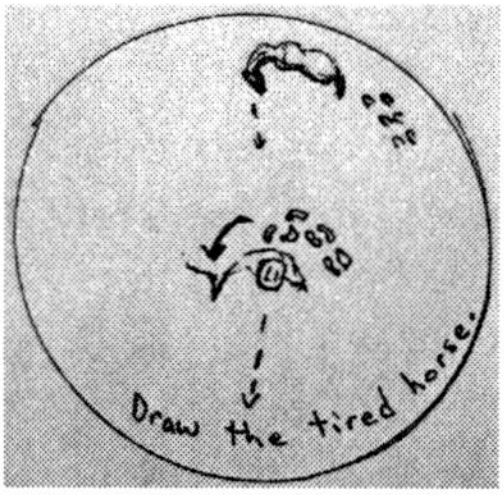

This is significant because at that point he gets to consider the fact that I am not trying to hurt him. So, by controlling the movement of his feet and then allowing him to rest without additional pressure I am now starting to build on trust. It is important that we do not run him to the point that he lathers up and his lungs explode. This would be extremely abusive and we would not get anything positive from the experience. In fact, it could work to teach him not to trust us. If you are not getting the signs of submission it may be better to simply change his direction in the circle more frequently rather than to "run the wind out of him".

When the horse has stopped and he is facing us. I turn toward the horses neck and gently (but not cautiously) walk toward his shoulder with the desire to rub his shoulder with a single stroke downward. Usually,in the beginning, as I get a couple feet away from the horse, he turns out and starts to run again. If he does then I make it my idea, toss the rope and I chase him on.

If he will not stand and let me to rub his neck then I will chase him off back to the rail again. When that happens I let him run 2 or 3 good laps and then move in on his neck and shoulder to pinch him off and chase him in the other direction. At this point I will usually see more dipping of the head and I will turn away to draw him back into the center again. This time as he comes in, I walk a few steps toward the opposite rail and then gently approach the horse and ask him to facing me. I usually move toward him in an arch pattern (arching away from his nose) letting his left and right eye get comfortable with my approach and retreat. I am not just rushing in on him at this point, I am giving him a better chance to succeed. However, if at any point, he walks away from me, I make it my idea and send him off again by raising my hand and shaking the lead rope towards his rear end. Make sure you are not in kicking distance when you do that. I only ask for a couple laps in each direction and let him back into the center for a rest. I ask for less laps because I do not want to blow him out, I just want him to dread having to go back on the fence and let him start realizing that he does not have to do it if he simply stands still and relaxes for me to take over.

Usually, by this time, I can approach the horses shoulder and give him that one rub (downward at the shoulder), and I can turn away and walk off about 6 paces away from the horse, come back and do it again. This again, helps the horse find confidence in the idea that I do not want to hurt him. And that I expect him to stand quietly when I approach. At this point the horse is also beginning to feel tired and he is looking for options. To stop running is one option that he is beginning to consider. Remember, that trust is easy to get, easier to loose and tough to regain, so do not over do the round pen chasing and do not

betray that trust by hurting this horse when he does quiet down and come back in.

I have seen people go to great lengths to catch their horse in the pasture and watched them scream and yell and beat the tar out of their horse when they do finally catch them, because they are so frustrated at that point, that they take it out on the horse. You do not need to be a horse whisperer to understand why that horse will probably not look forward to running up to you the next time you meet him in the pasture. Be smart about when and how you reward you horse for good or bad behavior. Every situation that involves a human and a horse involves a lesson of some type.

Sorry for the digression, at that point I clip the lead rope on the halter and begin to quietly lead the horse forward, backward, left and right. If he gets nasty, spooky, or fractious then I chase him off into the circling game again until he calms down and shows me signs of submission again.

The horse may start to realize that he is over-reacting, or that acting badly causes me to chase them off. In either case, they should start responding more calmly, that is a supportng requirement for my ability to take the leadership role. He is learning that I can control the movement of his feet.

In this program, I make sure to respond to good behavior with calm relaxing movement, and on the other hand I respond to bad behavior by making the horse work harder. The horse will start to walk nicely at my shoulder.

Horse Trainers Secret:

Make the right response from your horse easy (on the horse), and make the wrong response more difficult for the horse (more difficult but not painful)!

Good round pen work is a basic component in all Progressive Gentle Horse Training. If I do not have access to a round pen then I simple do the same work that I just mentioned but I keep the horse on a 14' to 20' lead rope, or I do the work in a small arena.

Once the horse is calm and following me reliably I will start to pet and rub the horses shoulder, back, neck and hind quarters. I alternate by leading him forward, backward, left and right then I go back to rubbing him down. The time spent here helps him build confidence in my leadership and faith in my gentle nature.

During short breaks in our sessions I spend time rubbing the horse's neck and head, getting him better about accepting my physical attention. By doing this we are beginning our despooking methods.

Consider the fact that despooking to certain things helps the horse relax and focus on the real cues that I'm giving them. If they are afraid of me or the brush in my hand, or a tarp on the ground, or the clippers, then asking them to stand quiet for that stuff is obviously an unreasonable expectation.

Despooking helps a horse to relax to things that would normally frighten him.

Groundwork and Despooking

When we start doing the groundwork program we should always lean toward building greater trust when the session ends. This is the basis and goal of all progressive training. The horse should do what we are teaching him with greater confidence, better calmness, and on a lighter cue.

Let us get started by simply leading the horse in a controlled environment (like a small paddock, arena, or round pen). I like using a rope halter and a 14' lead rope. I ask the horse to follow me without crowding me or running me over.

I expect the horse to walk forward patiently, walk backwards when I push on his nose and if I turn right or left I expect him to follow my lead there willingly. Of course, when he does not do it calmly it signals the opportunity to work on circles. By that I mean I chase the horse into a light lungeing exercise, in the circular pattern. I send him for just a few laps then I bring him back in and ask for another try.

It is my responsibility not to ask for too much too quickly. I never loose my patience because I know that he is going to get it eventually.

As the horse becomes good about leading, I give him a little rest with every break-through. As he becomes consistently better about it, I increase the challenge gradually. Here in lies the art work. Gradually I increase the work as he understands the prior lesson. This way we are always improving. If that next session is too big or too much, I go back to the previous lesson and avoid arguing with him. I find something less intimidating to work on, or, spend more time on that previous lesson.

In doing this, I progressively get the horse better about leading and also accomplish some despooking along the way. Despooking works to make the horse calmer and teaches him to rely on me when he does get scared or if he does not understand something. This helps us build our partnership.

In despooking, I will sometimes start by tossing a tarp on the ground and get the horse to work near the tarp. At first it's something that offers the horse concern. He does not want to get too close to it. He certainly does not want to touch it.

I do not just push him to cross it. Instead, I layout the tarp and longe the horse near it. Initially, the horse probably does not get any closer than 4 to 6 feet away. If the horse is worried about it you will see him turning his head at it and avoiding it as he passes by. So, I work progressively closer to the fringe of the tarp until his fear takes a subtle change for the better. That is when I let him rest near the tarp. If he runs off then I take him back on the circle. Pretty soon the horse starts to relax a little more around the tarp and appreciate the rest.

I will let the horse rest for a few minutes then lead him up to the tarp and back him away from it. I repeat that process several times until I feel his body language responding more calmly. On the third or forth introduction I'll lead him up and have him rest in front of the tarp. Basically, his fear should start turning into a curiosity. At first he might take the form of a sniff or two, then a bit later he might paw at the tarp a time or two. As his interest builds, I back him away from it and let him start building a stronger desire to come back to it. Most horses will.

Horses that have a healthy curiosity develop more quickly in their training than horses that appear completely uninterested in things that are new to them, or the horses that are completely bonkers about them. I use the same techniques for helping horses to over-come the fear of horse trailers as well.

Once the horse respects me and trusts that I am not going to hurt them, then all I really need to do is teach the horse a "move forward cue" and remain patient.

In teaching a move forward cue, I will tap him on the top of the rump with very light rhythmic pressure until he makes the slightest move in the right direction (it might be as subtle as a lean forward). I reward the horse by removing the pressure, or, on occasion, I will actually back him out of it. In a short time a horse that respects and trusts me will pick this up and remember it. He starts to learn that to relax to things I introduce him to.

In fact, one of the things I will do when helping someone find a training prospect is toss something (like a bucket or a jacket) in the pasture and see if the horse comes up to check it out. I try to steer away from the horses that over react as well as the horses that show no interest at all.

I am usually not done with the session until the horse crosses the tarp or enters the trailer at least three times willingly. I progress gradually until the horse is confident. Another point I would like to make is that I take 3 or 4 days on major hurdles. I try to work on it enough to leave the horse confident and consistent about our lesson.

Usually, tarps and water hazzards take about 20 to 30 minutes for a horse to get used to but a trailer can take 2 hours because it can be a much greater challenge for claustrophobic horses. By working with the horse patiently and progressively they build the kind of confidence that keeps them on a successful track.

I use stationary objects on the ground to help the horse learn how to develop their curiosity and confidence in my leadership as well as in things that are unfamiliar. Later, I progress to objects that move and make a noise, like bells, rattles, umbrellas, and whistles.

I spend time desensitising the horse to the lead rope by gently tossing it over his back. If the horse moves away I keep putting the pressure on. If the horse stops moving his feet and shows any sign of relaxing, I stop pushing him, the rest is a reward. A gently rub replaces the pressure stimulous. Soon he learns to relax around me.

The horse adopts a new way to look at things that are different. Things that would have been extremely scary in the past now seem a lot more interesting. Things that would have caused a panic attack and caused the horse to bolt away, now attract the horse with a new confident curiosity. That is when the learning curve starts to grow very quickly.

From the lead rope, I progress to rubbing the horse down with a small rag or if the horse is not too jumpy, I will use a plastic shopping bag, or even a long handled broom (like a push broom).

When desensitizing the horse to things by hand I always let the horse give it a look over and a quick sniff before I start rubbing it on the horses shoulder. Whether I am desensitizing the horse to a new curry comb, or a saddle, I follow the same routine. I start at the shoulder and I rub the horse with it, then, I progress to the horses withers and the base of the neck and work forward (higher on the neck) and backward, over the back, and finally over the rump and off the hip. Once the horse stands quiet and relaxed for the shopping bag, I tie the bag to the end of a 4' dressage whip.

I step away and move the bag and whip's end at a 45 degree angle away from the side of the horse in big sweeping movements. If the horse moves away from the bag then I keep his head tipped toward me and continue. If the horse stops moving his feet and starts to relax I slow down or stop completely. We call this flagging the horse.

<u>Important Note:</u> Whatever I do to one side, I must do to the other side as well. Horses need to see things from both eyes.

Once the horse will stand quiet for the flagging of the shopping bag on the whip, I work with a baby rattle at the end of a 4' stick and follow the same pattern of desensitization. Then, I progress to shaking a tarp or slicker jacket around the horse. If he gets too scared or spooked I will simply come back to something easier for the horse to handle.

It does not matter if we are trying to get a horse in a trailer or if we are trying to get a horse over spooky fences or if we are trying to shoot guns off the horses back. Once fear and bolting get replaced by curiosity and confidence the world gets a lot easier for the for you and your horse.

Inside of a few weeks horses can be lead through gun fire and flaming jumps, or taught to stand quietly below a helicopter. These things require patience and progressive training.

Remember the recipe for success.

1) Get the horses respect.
2) Get the horses trust that you will not hurt him or put him in any danger that he can not handle.
3) Then progress in your ability to coach the horse to understanding what you introduce him to, slowly , gradually, progressively.

If you introduce something too quickly and the horse explodes or over reacts, do not freak out. Instead, try to give the horse a little space and let him calm down then spend a little time on something he already knows. Work your way back up to it.

Safety is our top priority. Keeping a hand on the lead rope makes it fairly easy to keep the horses head bent toward you. As Clinton Anderson (a great and witty horseman) says ,"you can out run any horse that is looking at you". So, even if he wants to run off, you can keep the horses head bent toward you and control or at least limit the horses movement.

Creativity is the limiting factor here. Remembering that to keep things gradually progressive is very important. We need to start thinking in terms of "would a horse find this more scary or less scary than the last thing I did with him". Then Iwe can line things up in our mind from least scary to most scary. That will help us know what we should try next (it's progressive).

You should start with the least scary objects and then progress to the most scary objects.

If the horse seems excessively nervous or bothered by our work. You can back off and spend a little more time on something from the less scary part of the line up.

Important Note: If the horse acts scared or nervous I keep the stimulus / pressure going if the horse makes the slightest try to relax, I slow down, decrease, or remove the pressure. When the horses feet stop moving and the horse relaxes (licks and chews, cocks a leg, or takes a big exhale) I stop completely for a minute or two and just rub or pet him.

Once I have tried as much as I can think of, over several days, I set up the mounting block next to the horse or sit on the fence with the horse on a lead rope and I start waving flags and bags, etc, over the horses back. This desensization over the horses back is done to help the horse prepare to take a rider (some folks call this a preflight check).

Desensitizing horses helps them learn to develop a better / safer response to fearful situations.

Equine Preflight Check

The "Equine Preflight Check" is a term that is used by a lot of horseman. It is basically a system of testing or checking-out the horse before mounting him to ride. Remember in this book I am NOT teaching colt starting. This book is more about developing or perfecting the horse that has been ridden but has some issues.

The Preflight check helps you understand your horses mental and physical state or condition prior to mounting the horse that day. I know for a fact that making use of this technique can help everyone ensure that the ride they plan or want to have is a lot closer to the ride they are going to have. It could even save your life.

With as much time as I have spent with horses even I get surprised every now and then by a horse that shows lameness 30 minutes into a ride or a horse that gets into an argument leaving the property, or a horse that freaks out at a pile of tree limbs on the road and wants to run home. I should say that the number of times that this has happened to me would be a whole lot smaller if I took a little more time in the Preflight Check before every ride.

It is easy to see the value in this principle for a horse you have never ridden or the horse that you seldom ride, but I want to tell you that it is important even for your main (normally quiet) mount (the one you ride all the time). Sometimes, I can tell very quickly that my horse is ready and wants to take a ride with me. In those cases it takes less time. Sometimes, the preflight check becomes my training opportunity and instead of taking a long ride that day I do about an hour's worth of groundwork.

A sound preflight check program for a horse with a good head on his shoulders takes about 6 to 10 minutes. A green horse might take 15 to 30. A rank / nasty horse might take 30 ~ 60 minutes (and I may even decide not to ride depending on the course of events). So, hopefully that helps you keep things in perspective.

I will explain what I do in most cases:

The Preflight Check starts with catching the horse. If I go out to catch my horse in his pasture and he does not come running to me then I probably have a horse that would rather hang out with his pasture buddies. If he runs away from me I take advantage of the behavior and observe his movement. I am looking at his feet, legs, head, and top line. I want to see the top line moving fairly level and steady, if his head bobs with every other step on the forehand or the hip sinks on a certain step or if he is short on a certain stride, it is a good indication that he has got a physical lameness. If he just does not want to hang out with me, I take advantage of that desire to move away and actually encourage it. I will chase him off. I make it my idea, and push him away from me. Just as if I were free longeing the horse in the round pen, I chase him out. When he turns to face me and stops running I stop chasing him and turn away slightly. This is the same as taking the pressure off him. Soon horses learn that acceptance behavior is rewarded and they will come to you (while the pressure is off) to keep you from chasing them away. At the very least, I want the horse to stand still while I catch him and slide my halter and lead rope on him. Of course the bigger the pasture the longer this might take. If I catch him without a chase I give him a small treat (carrot or apple slice) and a nice rub, then I might longe him for a minute or two in both directions anyway to watch his movement.

If the horse looks lame I deal with it appropriately. I write down all the symptoms as I see them. I check breathing, temperature, heart rate, pulse, hydration (skin twist), and capillary refill time.

I also check the body for injury and the sensation of heat from a gloveless hand slowly passed over the skin. Obviously if the horse is lame we reschedule our trip for another day, and call your Vet.

If the horse is caught and he proves not to be lame, I will lead him around and test his willingness to follow me. I lead him forward backward left and right. I will toss my lead rope over his back and around his sides and legs and see if he is exceptionally spooky or quiet and controlled. I will brush him down and watch his ears and tail. If he is pinning his ears at me or smacking the heck out of me with his tail then I probably need to take a little time and confirm my leadership in his eyes by getting his feet moving. Next, I will lunge him a few times and get him going on my send and bend exercise (lunge him forward then brace the lead rope and make him swing his hip around as he runs out of rope).

When he is listening, I introduce the saddle pad and saddle him up gently. Here, again, I am watching for disagreement or quiet nature from the horse. Make sure to check your tack. Make sure it is sound, clean, strong and safe. You do not want to saddle a horse with a pad that has a small clay bee hive nested in it (I know because it has happened to me).

Make sure you do not tighten the girth too quickly, I like taking 3 or 4 gradual steps at tightening the girth. Horses get cinchy (irritated) about getting cinched if you have a tendency to tighten the cinch too quickly. Once I have the saddle on, I lunge him around one or two laps in each direction. To help him settle in his breathing. At that point I tighten the cinch again (on an exhale). Then, I bridle the horse and check all leather and the bit seat in the horse's mouth.

Once the horse is bridled, I stand at the left shoulder and hold the stirrup in my right hand and the lead rope or left rein in my left hand (Keeping the horses nose tipped toward me) and slap the stirrup fender on the side of the horse. I then change to the right side of the horse and do the same. If the horse acts spooky I keep it up until he calms down then I stop. The reward is the release of pressure. This helps the horse realize that he should relax when he is wearing a sadlle and I am by his side (he starts to trust that even though things are a bit scary, nothing bad is going to happen).

After working the stirrups and the saddle I will take my jacket or some ropes and wave them around the horse and pat the horses neck, the saddle, and the top of the hind quarters with the jacket.

Again, if the horse acts panicked then he is not ready to ride. If he calms down and stops moving his feet then I stop and do the other side.

This work does two things: It lets me check how spooky or irritated he is that day, and it also helps him to remember that, if he gets upset, or panicked, his best response is to relax and trust me.

I also take a few minutes and work on lateral flexion. Standing at the left side of the saddle, hold the left rein at the pommel or horn of the saddle in your right hand and slide the left hand down the left rein to about 8 to 12 inches from the bit and gently bring the horses head to the left. Hold the head to the left until the horse seeks his own relief by bringing his head even closer to you on the left. When he moves his head to the left and finds his own relief of pressure you should reward him with a release of the rein (immediately). Timing is critical, release must be immediate, after the horse makes the right move. Then do the same thing on the other side. This kind of groundwork almost always improves your control in turns and stopping the horses you ride.

By this time, if the horse is quiet, I prepare to mount. I check or tighten the girth one last time. Then I gather the left rein in my left hand, tip the horses nose slightly to the left, and hold a small handful of mane with the rein at the base of the horses neck, then I gently push the hip with my right hand to get the horse to widen his stance a bit to better support my weight, and with my left foot in the left stirrup I climb up while looking at the horses head.

With my right hand I will put my left foot in the left stirrup and step up in the stirrup. I try to get up and down twice before actually swinging my leg over the saddle. Again, I am watching for the horse's reaction and preparing him to be ridden. When he looks relaxed I will accept it as an invitation to climb aboard.

If the horse moves away I simply get down and work the horse in tight circles. Remember, that if he has the energy to move off while we are mounting then he is got enough energy to do a few push-ups (in the form of running tight circles). Make sure you work your horse enough to make him think it is better to stand quiet while you mount him.

When he is quiet, let him relax for a moment and mount the horse.

Most people at this point let the horse walk off as soon as they get on. This is a bad idea. It is much better to sit quiet and take a mental 30 count. Never start at a trot or canter. Your first mounted movement should always be flexion training or a slow walk, and only after a brief wait.

The first thing I like to do on the horses back is work on lateral flexion. I will ask for neck flexion to the left and right at least three times each before asking the horse to walk on.

Then spend two to five minutes at the walk with stops and turns and a few backup cues before asking for a trot. Then spend about 2 or 5 minutes doing the same thing at the trot before asking for a canter. After about 2 to 3 minutes at the canter, if everything has gone well, your horse is ready for the trail ride.

Do not ride the horse if the horse is not respectfully cooperating from the ground.

Green Horse & Green Rider Drills

For many years I've been helping horses and horse owners try to understand each other and get along better.

The majority of the calls I get are not to help an owner start a horse but rather the majority of calls I get are related to perceived problems with a horse's training. Sometimes it's a call about a head shy horse, sometimes it's a call about a horse who will not allow the farrier to handle his feet, sometimes it's about a horse that is buddy sour, or a horse that rears. Inevitably, the majority of problems relate to a lack of experience for the horse, the rider, or both.

A while back, I developed a program that helps people and horses build on their confidence and experience with a little help from a friend. I find that when the horse is inexperienced he needs more time in a controlled environment with consistent training from a confident rider.

Similarly, when the horse has problems that are related to fear, what they really need is to slow down a bit. We can help them best by doing things in a more progressive nature, in a more controlled environment, with greater consistency. In those situations, they may benefit by being handled by a more confident leader.

In many cases, the rider simply needs more time in a controlled riding experience that helps them build confidence, saddle balance and clear communication signals.

Sometimes, when I go out to help a horse what I end up finding out is that the horse is actually fairly well balanced in his training but because the rider was either less experienced or a bit afraid the signals that the horse was receiving were misleading or, in some cases, counter productive.

Let's see if I can expand on this a bit?

The first thing I do is get people working their horse on a circle. Why a circle? Well, the idea is that there are no corners to get hung up in. Since controlling the horse requires getting control of the feet, we need to know that when we send a horse in a certain direction that they can continue to move without obstruction until we ask the horse to do something else.

If the horse runs to a corner, it is easy for him to get stuck or confused and start thinking about his choices without our help. The circle also allows us to stand in the center, or if on the horses back, work on the rail and keep the movement flowing.

If the horse runs for a mile and he still can't lose us, or even exhaust us in the process, he starts to learn respect for our persistence and stamina. Now, I don't mean to say that he is too small minded to realize that we do not have to move because we are in the center of the circle, but, the outcome is the same.

When we can effectively control his movement and direction he will gain better confidence in our leadership and respect us more for it (works 99% of the time).

This is also the kind of work that inevitably helps the horse build confidence on the circle work itself. He becomes more confident at the walk, trot, and canter while we work him from a rope (lunge line), on the circle. If he is more confident, that means that he is less fearful. As we work the horse in the controlled area on the circle we also become more confident in his ability to behave and understand us.

So, confidence is growing in both of us, in this type of training!

If we pay close attention to the horse when we work with him (on that circle), we can start to understand his body language a little better. We can see when he is nervous, excited, tired, angry, or not very cooperative. This is really important stuff to know about (in the horse you plan to ride).

Working with a strange horse is easier with the help of a friend.

Here is a fact that I like to make use of: People that love horses have friends that love horses.

My program for helping Green horses and Green riders makes use of this fact. Again, what I do is spend a little time helping a handler work a horse on a circle from a 22' lead or lunge line.

Once that person (ground handler) is working well from the center (he can control forward movement and bring the horse to a stop or an inside turn with little effort), then we can stop the horse and have the rider climb aboard. This allows the rider to spend a little more time as a passenger without having to control the horse. The rider learns to balance in rhythem with the horse's movement. The rider gets to capture that "Feel in the saddle". The horses get more practice taking a rider under controlled circumstances. It is a great way to build confidence for both the horse and the rider.

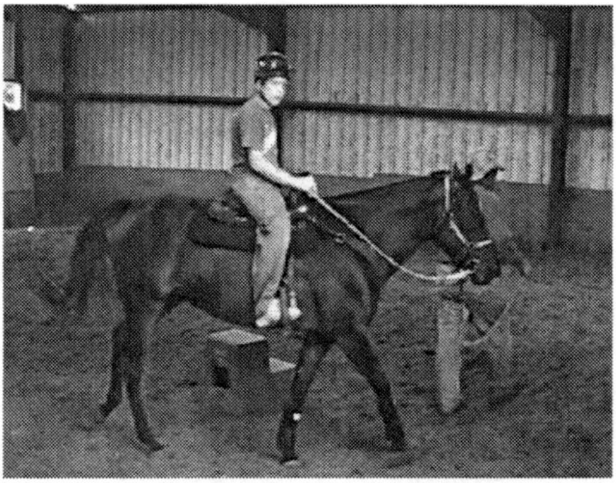

How long we spend on this drill depends on progress and confidence of both horse and rider. Too little time and progress is challenging and difficult. It creates anxiety and nervous tension. Too much time, and things start to get boring and slow. The horse may begin to lose his exuberance and desire to continue.

As we continue to progress with this confidence building exercise we can add things like cavaletti, or a low 12" jump. We can also add a bridle and reins and let the rider start controlling the

Go and the Whoa. Of course, having a friend on the other end of the lead rope means that you always need to make inside turns (always turning toward the inside of the circle).

Pretty soon, the rider can start working on figure eights, stopping, backing up, etc., with confidence! You can work on gate transitions (walk to trot, trot to walk, walk to canter, canter to trot, etc.). The situation offers the safety of having a friend on the line. All the while the horse is starting to learn the riders body language, the riders cues, the way the rider asks for a turn, a stop, a back, etc.

Sometimes in early training the person on the ground can help the horse understand the rider better by re-enforcing your requests from the ground. If the horse will not initiate a trot from a leg squeeze, the ground person can reinforce the cue with a swing of a dressage whip or the end of the rope. Once

confidence and control are fully restored between the horse and the rider then the well grounded buddy can help by providing assistance with mounted despooking.

Mounted DeSpooking

In every horse there is an accident waiting to happen. We can not expect an animal, as vulnerable as a horse, to respond to everything he is exposed to with perfect confidence without special training.

There are a lot of horse trainers out there that have very successful training methods for dealing with spooky horses. There really are so many different methods and techniques for dealing with this that I could never cover them all.

We all know that for hundreds of years the horse was an integral component of battle. Mounted soldiers and hunters are a large part of our history, so these things are not new. We can say, with confidence, they are very possible to achieve.

Horses can be confident loyal soldiers that carry us through battles, with flaming arrows, lances, gun fire and loud explosions. Even though we all know that this is true, we often feel extremely apprehensive to work on despooking our horses. Some horse trainers even go public to say that it isn't a good idea to desensitize or despook horses, for fear of inspiring dullness.

Personally, I spend some time on despooking with every horse I work. To me, it is not so important that I desensitize the horse to everything the horse could encounter. However, I do need to teach how to react to fear. The whole purpose to my desensitizing horses (mounted or from the ground) is to teach them that the best way to respond to something that scares them, is to simply relax, observe it, and trust in my leadership.

> **NOTE ON SAFETY**: Before doing any despooking while mounted you need to make sure that the horse has received the same type of despooking without a rider.

These things take time!

Avoid frightening the horse into a dangerous explosion. It is best accomplished by the progressive methods that we have already discussed.

Line things up in accordance with how scary you think they will be and start with the least scary object first and progress into more scary objects. If you make a mistake and something that you are introducing is actually scarier to the horse than you thought it would be, then put it away until you think the horse is ready for it. Go back to a previous object, spend a little more time at that level and progress to something else on your "next scary thing list".

Another important thing to remember is that despooking is the process of introducing a stimulus that makes the horse nervous or slightly afraid. When the horse responds correctly, by looking at, but not moving away from the object, then you remove the stimulus (slow it down, make it quieter, or take it away completely).

Many horseman have heard of sacking out a horse as being the process for desensitizing horses. It is a common misconception that the process involves shaking bags on a horse that is snubbed up to a post that will not allow escape, and continuing the stimulous until the horse is completely numb to it. That process might work but it is a very dangerous approach to horse training. If it is done improperly the horse can be injured and equipment can be destroyed, and a horible reaction can be learned by the horse.

Along with asking the horse to respond correctly we also work on simple riding during the process of despooking. In other words, we might ask the horse to do some figure eights at one side of the arena while someone is roiling or bouncing a 5 foot rubber ball at the other end of the arena, or while someone blows a whistle at the other end of the arena. Allow the horse a 30 to 60 second look at first, then ask him to pay attention to us and our mounted patterns.

The better the horse trusts and respects the rider the quicker he learns to relax on the battle field. Never try to beat him over a fear or distraction. This is a common mistake. When a horse balks. Some people will kick their horse with hopes of getting him over it. It is far better to get him working hard at something that he will do and bring him back to that thing that he would not do after he gets a little tired of the previous activity. If he balks again then take him back to do what he will do. If the horse has got the energy to do the wrong thing then he certainly has got the energy to work on the right thing. This is why beating a horse into a trailer is a bad idea, it works against his desired behaviour and breaks his trust in you.

The way we do it at Black Steed Acres is to allow the horse to get a little afraid of a stimulus (flag on a stick, a rattle on a stick, a small tarp waiving in the air, a cap gun, clippers, etc.), and the moment that the horse looks at it, stops moving his feet, and shows any sign of even the slightest relaxation, we take the stimulus away (rewarding the slightest try).

The horse learns to trust us and relax. He may actually be afraid, but he learns that a relaxed response makes the frightening thing go away.

The better he gets at this training the more we can introduce. Soon we can shoot guns and bows off the horse's back.

This flag on a stick is a great tool in any barn.

Getting Better Control

Occasionally, I will get a call to work with a horse that is fairly well behaved but does not do "some things" very well. Whether he is hard to stop or turn, he does not move laterally very well, he doesn't maintain his gaits, his transitions are weak, or he does not turn a nice circle, etc. I work the same program on them all. I believe that a good foundation takes care of everything.

When I get on the horses back I usually find some obscurity in his patterns and sensitivity. By putting first things first, everything gets progressively better. After even just just a little time the horse starts moving better. This is often the result of a soft handed, confident rider. A rational minded horse will progress quickly with a savvy confident rider. So, fixing (fine tuning) the horse is helpful but it will usually prove ineffective in the long run if we do not follow up with appropriate rider training.

I see this most often with “neck reiners”, because they have learned to simply pull the rein to the right or left and they expect the horse to (in simple terms) respond. I do see it in direct reiners as well, but more often in neck reiners. Most riders do not take the time to feel it from the horse's perspective (put themselves in their horses shoes).

This can be fixed! If there is one thing that I have learned it is that horses (like people) often require a slightly different feel or pressure for proper stimulation. That difference (in my opinion) is much smaller for horses than for humans, but sometimes you need to do a little fishing to find the right feel. For instance, from the moment you get on the horse, some horses expect a clear signal to move forward before they consider taking a single step, some start moving the moment your foot hits the stirrup.

I approach every horse the same way in training them, and make small adjustments (as needed), as we progress together. Once I get the right response (a better response), I start transferring the signal to the way “it should feel”. Once the horse is confident about what my signals mean (I can tell because he starts to relax when I ask for something). Once I get the right response I start working on consistency. This is what I call refinement work.

Refinement is all about consistency. If the horse is trained to refinement but the rider is not, then every time the rider mounts the horse, he will add a certain amount of confusion to those well defined signals and begin diffusing the sensitivity of that cue.

Sometimes an ill prepared rider can completely frustrate a well trained horse and it shows up as attitude on the horses part, which usually gets treated with more attitude from the rider. That is when the partnership starts to break down. Like that snowball that rolls downhill, it just keeps getting bigger (worse in this case). With that knowledge it is easier to understand why you need to spend some time on this.

Of course, I see a lot of horses that are not well trained and the rider is very quick to accept responsibility and blame for the failed partnership. I am happy to train the horse but it is not a partnership if one partner has trouble understanding or respecting the other.

When the horse is ready to take a rider, I like to spend a minute or two reminding the horse to walk, trot, canter, turn, stop, and back, before I head out on any trail ride. I focus on making my signals as clear as possible. If I am riding a strange horse I must spend a lot more time doing that than if it was one of my own horses. Whether I can ride in a arena or plan to take a trail ride, this work will help improve the experience. Whether we like to here it or not, every rider is a horse trainer (good or bad). Every ride is a training session (good or bad).

Let me take a few minutes to explain exactly how I approach this and what I do when things do not feel right.

1. **Stand while mounting.** No horse is ready to work if he can't stand still. If your horse takes the slightest step while mounting then start there. Set him up for success before you try to mount. Square him up so that he has a good footing. Start with a mounting block. I can get high above the horses back without climbing up. I simply walk up the step and raise my hand up and rub him. Reward him by leaving him be and by looking down or away slightly when he stands quiet(take some pressure off of him). Keep him on the lead rope at first. Progress to getting up and down as previously described until he will stand quiet every time. Make sure he doesn't take a single step for 30 seconds when you get up there. This might take a day or a week of practice but it will prove itself to be one of your most important training sessions as you get started. Many people get in big trouble when they are getting up or down off the horse.

2. **Lateral flexion.** Ask that horse to yield a light flex of the neck (bend the head around to the right and left) without moving it's feet. The horse should remain calm when you ask for

flexion. When he does then you know he's no longer afraid of the request to turn and he understands the signal and it's meaning. Follow the training previously mentioned and get good flexion before every ride.

3. **Walk Forward Cue.** When you are finally ready to walk forward you will ask for the walk. That means your butt is settled in the saddle, your legs are appropriately positioned in the stirrups and you have good rein management. At that point lean slightly forward, look to where you want the horse to go and gently squeeze with the lower part of your calf on both sides of the horse and begin a gentle rhythm in your hips to encourage forward motion. If the horse is a hot one and he picks up a trot I would suggest you sit back in the saddle, stop your seat movement and apply a one rein stop. Once he is settled, ask again. No horse is any better than his walk. By leaning forward and moving your seat, you are helping to make the signal clear. These things

will help you in the long run. The better you are at this work the better you will be at gate transitions from stop to walk and from walk to stop. You want to start with gentle encouragement and increase pressure progressively until he responds with forward movement every time. Avoid kicking the horse or smacking him very hard with a whip. Stay rhythmic, and progressive. If you are experiencing a lot of trouble get some help from a ground partner on a 20' lead rope. The idea is to spend as little time as possible in frustration and as much time as possible in signal clarity. Practice those transitions often and make sure that you are doing it the same way every time. As your signals become more clear the stress that your horse will feel decreases and your partnership will be much improved. As you develop excellence then you can start refining that walk to 3 different speeds (slow, medium, and fast walk). If the horse does not get it right, stop him or circle him down (tighter circles will slow the pace). When he gets it right, take a few strides and then let him rest as you pet him (pet not pat). Pet the horse and reassure the horse that he has done a nice job. Use that tone of voice that you always use when he has done something great.

4. **Walk to trot transitions.** This is an important phase of training because this will help your horse to ride well at a very popular business pace. I like to start with a gentle half halt signal (a wake up call to suggest that something is going to change). Start to trot by

positioning your seat at the forward area of your saddle, gently squeeze the lower leg (both sides of the horse) while you give a small cluck or kiss, and begin a short post. If the horse does not trot tickle the rump with your crop. When the horse picks up the trot let him take a couple strides then transition back down to a walk by dropping you seat position gently, reducing your hip action, and (if necessary) check the reins gently to a downward transition. Push your heels down and forward to help promote the feel of the transition. This will get better and better as you practice it. In a week of calm transition training, your horse will become very clear on the signals for requested movement (remember to reward good response and put a little extra work on a poor response). Do not fight with the horse! If he does not understand your request try a simpler request. Be creative, get your ground partner back on the long line to assist you, stay calm and work on signal clarity. Once he gets good at the transitions then start working on getting 3 speeds at the trot (slow, medium, and fast).

5. **The canter.** The canter is the gait that most people have some trouble with. I think it is because we are moving so much faster and the pattern is a lifting one that it makes us feel insecure and we tend to srespond by queezing into the saddle, and grabbing onto the reins for better balance and control. I often see people hold onto the saddle horn for safety as well which works against them in balance and control. I think a horse should pick up a

canter calmly and rhythmically without excitement from horse or rider. That takes confidence from both partners. Confidence takes practice (it is a simple formula). I do not progress to a canter until I have quiet walk and quiet trot transitions (upward and downward). I like to start the horse on canter work in a arena or enclosed pasture to contain the distance and safety factor. I will start my transitions from the walk (walk to canter then canter to walk). I get the horse on the rail and as we start to come out of a turn I will lightly brace the inside rein (keep it from turning in or out - without pulling to signal a stop). Then I will pull gently on the outside rein (pointing the tip of horses nose to the rail (just for a millisecond), with no movement yet from leg or seat (the idea is to make him feel a bit boxed in or claustrophobic), and then (at the moment the horse feels like he wants out of the box) I let out the outside rein, open up the inside rein (drawing the nose slightly to the inside by pulling the inside rein to the inside) and opening the virtual gate so that he can move quickly through it, and (at that moment) I give a squeeze with the outside leg behind the girth (startling him slightly to move him out). If he picks up a nice canter on an inside lead we go a few strides and I reward him (let him rest). If not, then we transition him back down and try again. If the horse does not take the inside lead in front and back legs then something is off balance (start with more inside nose and outside leg). Get your ground partner to help you if you need it. If the horse simply does not get it then try getting the horse going the opposite direction on the rail and turn him gently (into the rail) and as he straightens out from the turn, cue the canter. This will further expand on that claustrophobic nature and inspire bigger movement from the horse's inside lead. Remember not to get upset if things are not working out, instead further break it down or spend more time working on what he does know. This kind of work can inspire a certain amount of fear in the horse, and the thing that you should be focused on is getting his calm response from a lighter cue.

6. **Turning**. Turning is not just a reining issue. Start on the front end, then work on the hind quarters and lastly get the turn from the rib cage or the barrel of the horse (moving him straight to the side).
    1. **Turning on the front end.** I like to start by asking for exact movement from the horse's front legs. Starting from the halt, brace the left rein (the intent is to keep him

from moving the front left leg forward or back), you can further assist by putting his left legs on the rail, very gently use the right rein to the right side until he will move his right front leg one step to the right. Reward the slightest try (even if you just see the right knee lift slightly). If he feels like he wants to move forward then pull a soft stop, as he thinks about it, and adjust the position of the right rein until it becomes clear in his mind that the right front leg is the one that should move. It needs to go to the right. Work this drill on both sides of the horse. You can and should further assist by pushing slightly with the opposite leg (just in front of the girth). At first the horse is going to think the leg movement means that he should move forward so, use it as a signal booster once he starts to understand. Start with a light leg press then bump it rhythmically and directly to encourage faster movement. I like for rhythmic legs to mean "go faster". This will help him develop clarity and confidence and it will help you learn the feel of your horse. If he walks off don't get upset just try again. Remember to make over him when he gets it right. As he gets better at it, see if you can make it happen away from the fence. This will greatly improve your riding skills on that horse.

2. **Turning on the hind quarters**. This is a critical component of riding because this will get a horse to disengage his hind quarters in movement and act as a boat's rudder in steering your horse. This will also strongly improve your skill and control of the horse. Start by asking the horse to take one step to the right by pressing your leg on the left of the horses rib cage well behind the girth line. Keep the reins in a position that clearly indicates to the horse that you do not want to move forward (make sure you are not asking him to backup either), press gently with the left leg, and progressively increase pressure with a gentle, steady, rhythmic bump of your left leg. Stop immediately and reward the horse when he takes the slightest step to the right with his right hind leg. You can get some help from your ground partner in the early stages of this training. The idea is to put in your horse's mind that he needs to move away from the leg pressure and not confuse the signal with any other movement. Then get the horse walking on the rail, as he moves off

gently bring his nose into the rail and apply your outside leg pressure rhythmically pushing the 180 degree turn from the hindquarters. Reward the slightest try. Let him rest when he gets it right, keep trying (without getting upset) if he has a little trouble understanding.

3. **Turning on the rib cage – Straight Lateral movement.** This is one that many people have trouble with. It is really nothing more than a combination of turning the front, then the back, then the front, then the back and then, as he starts to move sideways, bump the center of the rib cage and steady the reins as he moves laterally. Reward the slightest fully lateral movement (straight move to the side). This is time well spent, as the horse learns to relax to your signals he will begin to progress more quickly.

7. **Stopping.** I can't think of too many things I would consider more important than stopping. If your horse is the kind that runs off and requires all the strength in your body over a period of 20 to 30 seconds to get him to stop then (holy cow), work on that first. I put it in this book as the 7th thing to work on because I like to have good control and confidence on forward movement and turning before I start asking for straight backing. I like to start by getting a perfect "One Rein Stop". I have already talked about that so, I will not spend a lot of time on that in this chapter.
To improve the straight stop, I walk the horse to a fence line and act as though I was going to apply a one rein stop (near the fence) and simply apply some supporting outside rein (to balance the gentle tug), as I sit down on the top of my back pockets and push my heels down and forward. The fence helps the horse realize that he can not go forward. I reward the slightest try and repeat the program over period of about 10 or 15 minutes, and, over several days until he seems to anticipate what I am asking for. I practice a bit in every session until he stops on a dime with extremely light rein pressure. Of course, as he gets better at it work him away from the fence, and eventually in the open pasture. If your horse has a tendency to take the extra steps when stopped in the center of the arena then get him to take one or two steps back every time you ask him to stop. Pretty soon he will anticipate the need to back and he will actually stop quicker. Reward the horse when

he gets it right. Do not fight with the horse. If he start showing real signs of frustration or anger then put him to work doing things that he can do rather easily.

8. **Neck Reining**. Do yourself a favor and get the signals clear from direct reining before you teach him the neck reining. Once he is working from calm clear signals then you can start with neck reining. Approach it in the same way but realize that where you apply the neck rein pressure on the neck and the angle of your tug (draw) will have a great deal to do with what he learns and how quickly he develops consistency.
9. **Precise Control (Cost and Benefit).** Remember that the more acute your controls become the more explicit your horse expects them to be. This can be a severe challenge for him if you put a sloppy rider on your well trained horse's back. That rider might be asking for a hundred different precise movements (unknowingly) and the horse gets punished (by the rider)with harsh, aggressive verbal tones, rough leg and seat manipulations or even some whip action, from the rider.

Improving controls is about practicing transitions over and over and making the signals (Cues) softer and lighter until horse and rider are invissibly speaking impeccably. It will cost you a lot of wet saddle blankets (it doesn't happen ver night).

Making Things Perfect

As we develop our relationship with our horses, our sense of responsibility and confidence as trainers, and we improve our efficiency as a horseman, we will begin to perfect our horse / human relationships. This is what I call making things perfect.

I often hear about people looking for a horse that does not need any training, the buyer wants to buy a perfect horse. There are many perfect horses out there and when those horses find a savvy (knowledgeable) horseman a perfect relationship comes quickly. Even in those situations there is a period of time when the horse learns to listen to the subtle differences of a handler's cues and they learn subtle differences in what the human expects as a desirable response. At the same time, the handler is learning the subtle difference in what makes the horse respond to what they want as a desirable response to their cues.

A person that has very little understanding in what makes a horse move and how to refine a horse's behavior will always find this challenging. Even a trained horse will be confused by an owner that squeezes his legs to feel more secure in the saddle, or someone who pulls on the reins to find better balance in his seat.

Eventually, a well trained horse will disregard his good training and try to understand the lunatic rantings of the unqualified rider. Frustration is an expected result when cues no longer have any consistency and they no longer seem to matter. The horse, under the heavy handed un-orthodoxed rider often feels like he's being punished for no reason by the person who is yanking on the bit or repeatedly kicking at their ribs. Soon the horse is back at a trainers barn because they are perceived as having a problem. Not too surprisingly, he is happy to be there.

A better approach to this work, is for the human (handler) to receive some training from an experienced trainer on a well schooled horse. This will help the human to better understand appropriate pressures, signals and cues to receive an appropriate response. This offers both the horse and the human a perfect start to making things perfect, it prepares the human for improving responsiveness from their own horse. They learn how to hold the reins and how to ask for a leg yield and how to feel a proper lead change, etc. Spending a little money here will help you get a lot further with your own horse later. And it can be a lot of fun!

You don't need years of training, few month or two should do the job (significant improvement). Once the human knows exactly how to cue the horse appropriately and work at it until they get a particular response then the only thing left to do is to work on it (repetition).
The human begins to work on it rather crudely at first and as the horse begins to understand what the rider is asking for, the rider can work on making the cues more and more subtle.

The goal is to have an effortless, imperceptive cue that the horse can sense or feel and, in response, the horse offers a desired reaction to that cue. Many things can get in the way of these efforts, such as fear (of something related or unrelated), and sensory confusion. In every case, the human that remains patient, persistent, and progressive is the one that finds perfect results sooner than the rest. This is the key to Progressive Gentle Horse Training and probably the key to your eventual success.

Take the time it takes! Many great trainers have said it.

By that we mean plan on riding the horse between 3 to 6 days a week to make him perfect. Work on a couple different things every time you ride. When you discover a problem spend a little time on it.

<u>For instance:</u> If you want a better trail horse, figure out (in your own mind), what that means to you. Maybe you want a horse that will not balk at the water crossing or a horse that will turn on a lighter cue, or a horse that will not change or break gate until asked to do so. With that idea, work on the water crossing, or turning responsiveness, or gait consistency, several times in every session.

I try to make absolutely sure that I am not expecting more than I should consider reasonable progress before I get started. Even if he did things better yesterday, do not get upset about set backs. Consider set backs an opporunity for training. In other words, I would not expect to make progress with my horse in crossing a bridge if he can not successfully walk across a sheet of plywood on the ground.

The other thing I must remember is that if I start something that gets a bad result, I should break down the steps to a simpler objective that will get me closer to my initial goal. At that point, I work on being consistent and persistent until the horse improves in some way. I try never to expect too much and I never quit without some improvement. In that way, the horse learns with at least some confidence that I am asking for communication and response, and he understands it a bit better than when we started.

It is foolish to think that riding a horse for 1 hour a week is going to improve his skills or yours with any significance. Making a perfect horse is a labor of love that requires time, patience, and skill. If you have these things working for you and you can dedicate 3 to 6 days a week, your horse will likely perform to a perfect level in about 4 to 8 months of work. If you can only work one day a week then put more time in (go 4 to 6 hours). If you do one day a week then do longer days of easier work. The different level at which the horse or the rider starts will affect the reality of that statement. An International champion dressage horse may take longer than a family loved trail horse, and the scrutiny of that definition will vary accordingly. You can count on your perfect horse (Nationally competitive) taking somewhere between 6 months to 2 years of training 3 to 6 days a week. You might never see that accomplishment if you ride a couple times a month.

Confirmation and Character also have a lot to do with actual success for horse or rider. If either one of you are not fit for the type of work you plan to do then it will never work out as well as you hope. If you make sure that your work is fun and progressive then you will never waist your time trying. As a last resort or possibly a first resort, do not rule out consulting an expert along the way, it may help keep you on track with your goals.

Horsemen are loosing ground every year in where we can ride and enjoy our horses. I hope you all find this book helpful and I pray that you all join your local or state horse council to ensure that the Horse does not lose his rights and place in our Society. Help us all preserve our right to ride.

We, at Black Steed Acres, pray that all your horses become perfect for you and that you thoroughly enjoy their presence in your lives through a fun, safe, progressive partnership.

What are you waiting for?
Get out there and start playing with your horses.

Take Care and God Bless!

Contact Joe Roa at:

joeroa@Blacksteedacres.com to qualify your mare for breeding with Joe's Perfect Friesian Stallion "Bjorn".

Visit
http://www.BlackSteedAcres.com/Bjorn.html

for more information.

364775

Made in the USA